AF255601

# Views From My KALEIDOSCOPE

# Views From My KALEIDOSCOPE

MELISSA A. MITCHELL

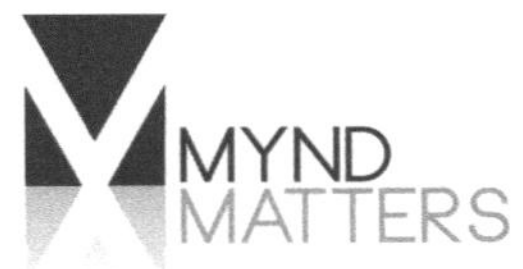

Published by Mynd Matters Publishing
201 17th Street NW
Suite 300,
Atlanta, GA 30363
www.myndmatterspublishing.com


Identifiers:
Library of Congress Control Number: 2017962503

ISBN-13: 978-1-948145-02-2 (pbk)
ISBN-13: 978-1-948145-03-9 (hdbk)


FIRST EDITION

*I dedicate this work to the woman
who chose to see love through her pain,
who chose to focus on light in her darkness,
who chose to seek the Spirit for comfort,
who chose to own her truth in the midst of confusion.*

*I dedicate this work to my former self.
We made it queen and there is no turning back!*

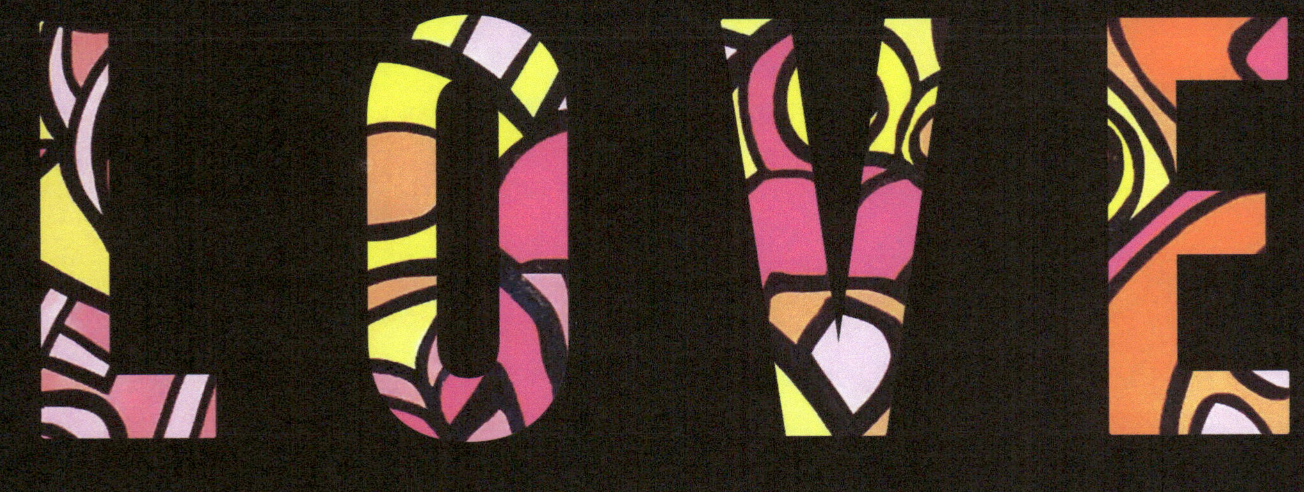

Let love transform even the darkest parts of you.

Love is stronger
than any mistakes that
you've ever made.
Love allows forgiveness.
Love keeps no records
of wrong doing.
Love conquers all.
God loves you,
don't ever doubt it
for one second!

If a person willingly gives of their time and access to their emotions, they certainly deserve consistency. Don't take people for granted, they need you more than you know.

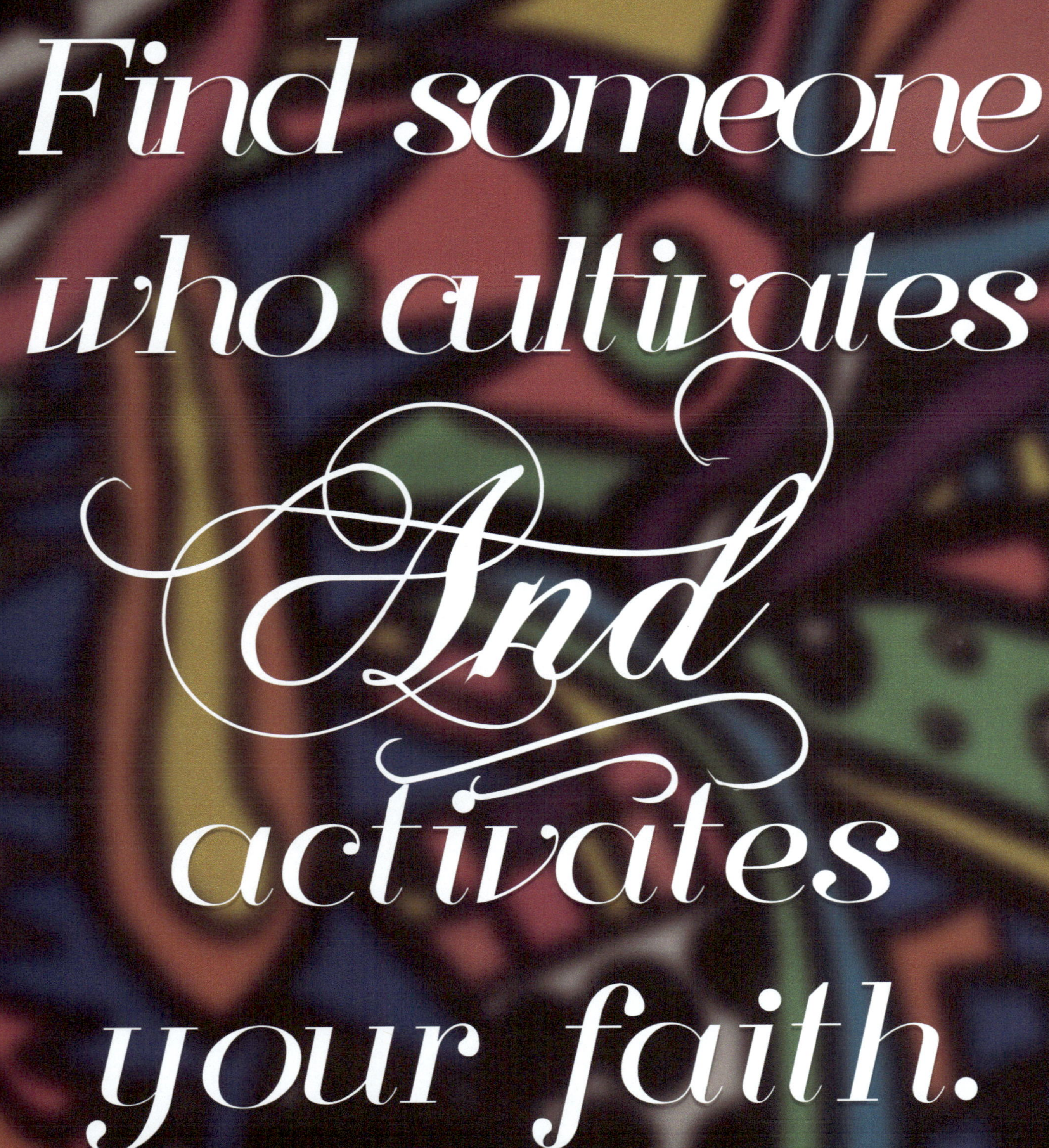

Find someone
who cultivates
And
activates
your faith.

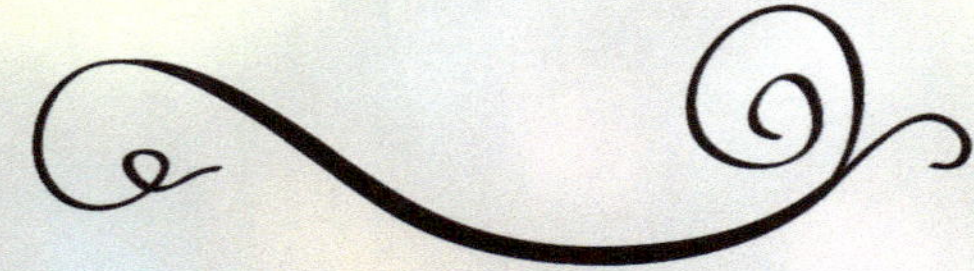

# WHEN CONNECTED TO THE RIGHT PERSON, YOUR PURPOSE CAN BE IGNITED AND MAGNIFIED.

WITH THE WRONG
PERSON, YOUR PURPOSE
CAN BE EXTINGUISHED
AND DIMINISHED.
BE CAREFUL WHO YOU
PICK AS IT WILL DIRECTLY
IMPACT YOUR DESTINY!

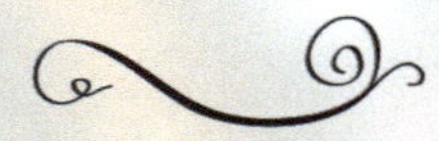

Stop
regretting
and hiding behind
your darkness. Every
part of your story makes
you unique. God crafted
your narrative to encourage
someone else to keep going.
If you've survived,
it's your duty to
help someone
else do the
same.

When you decide to
follow your purpose,
you must also be willing
to walk away from
some people.

When God allows something or someone to leave your life, He always finds a way to replace it. Sometimes it's even an upgrade. Just let Him do His thing

GOD
ALWAYS HAS
A BETTER VERSION
OF WHAT YOU THOUGHT
YOU WANTED
AND NEEDED.

In a relationship, you can only build a solid foundation if the other person also has building blocks in their hands.

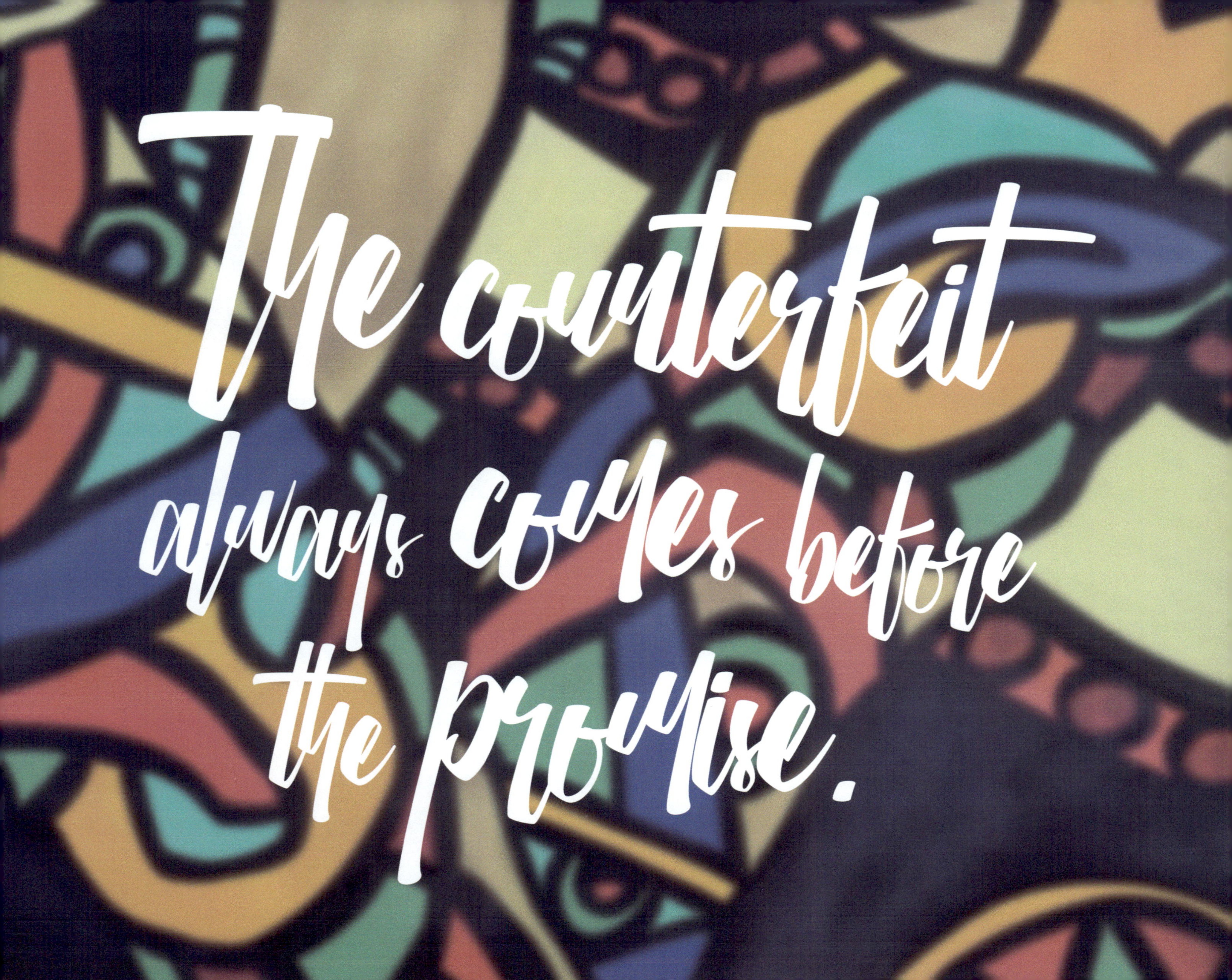
The counterfeit always comes before the promise.

Don't let anything
or anyone jeopardize
what you've prayed and
worked hard for.

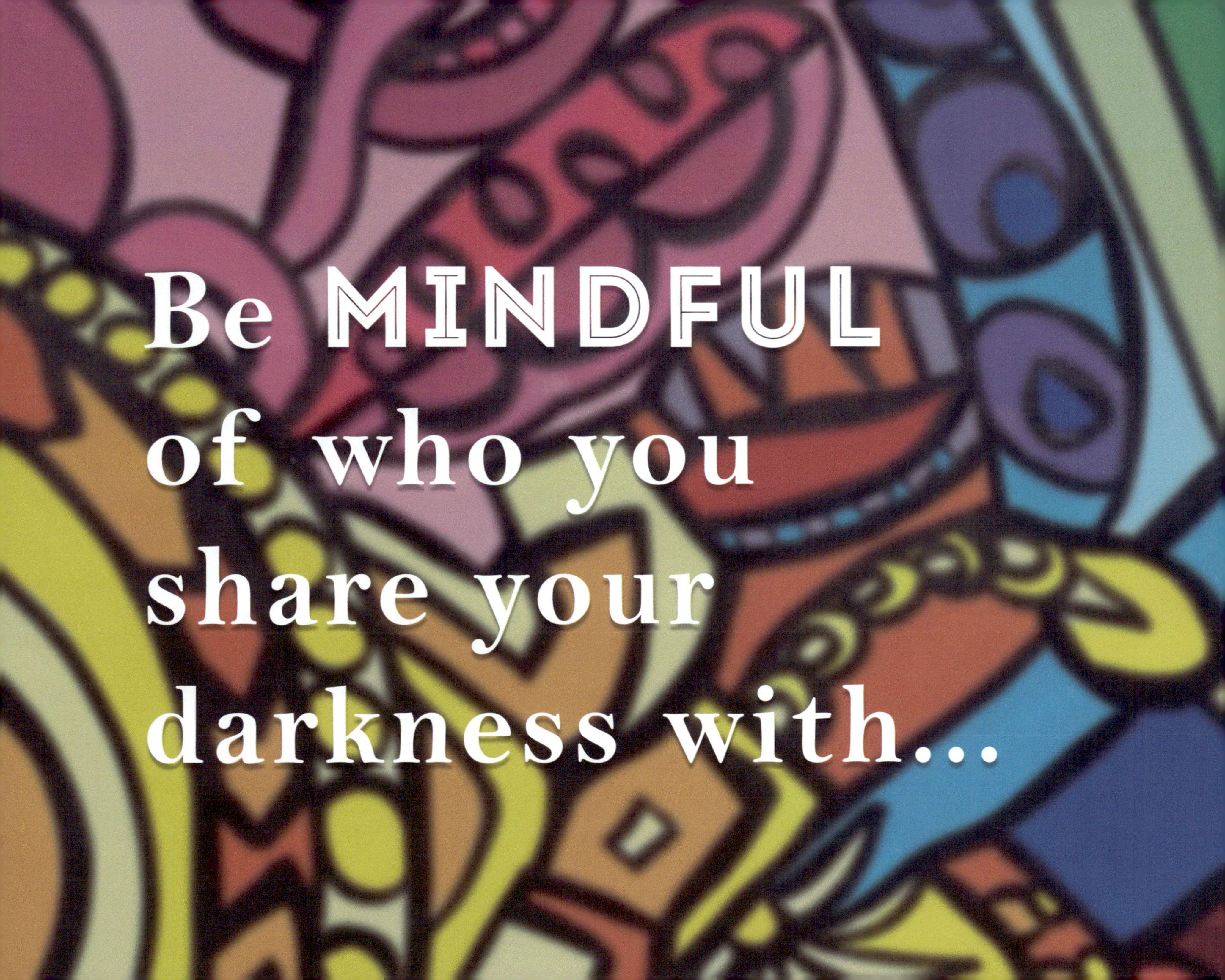
Be MINDFUL
of who you
share your
darkness with...

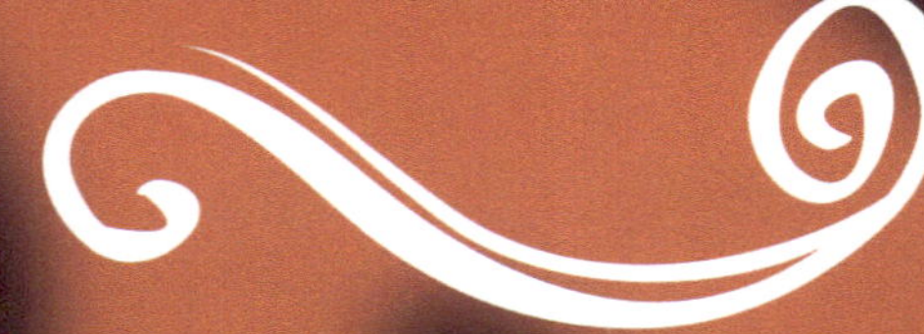

# DON'T SETTLE FOR BUTTERFLIES; SEEK A LOVE THAT RUNS DEEP TO THE CORE OF YOU.

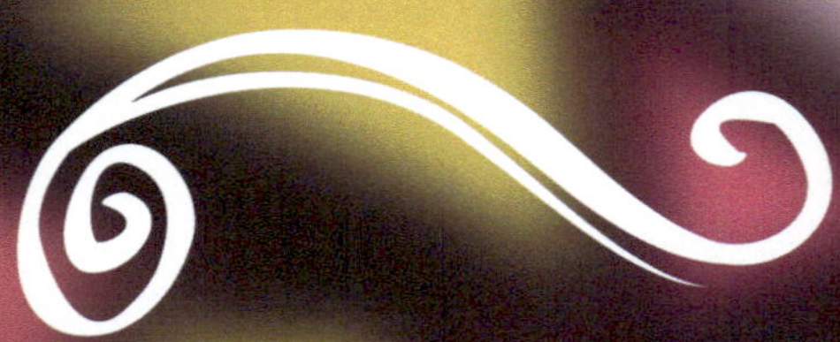

YOUR LOVE STORY DOESN'T HAVE TO MAKE SENSE TO OTHERS. IT IS WRITTEN IN A LANGUAGE THAT ONLY YOU AND YOUR SIGNIFICANT OTHER CAN UNDERSTAND. *STOP* TRYING TO EXPLAIN YOUR LOVE AND ALLOW LOVE TO EMANATE FROM YOU. AN ORDAINED LOVE CAN BE A WITNESS TO THE WORLD.

FIND
SOMEONE
WHO LOVES THE
SEED OF YOU AND
NOT JUST THE FRUIT.
EVERYONE DOESN'T DESERVE
THE BEST YOU. GOD HAS
DESIGNED SOMEONE
WHO IS WILLING
TO WATCH YOU
GROW.

TRUE
FRIENDSHIP
PERSONIFIES
THE
DEFINITION
OF
UNCONDITIONAL
LOVE

Some people **HAD** to leave your life so the overflow could be released.

LOVE IS HAVING UNCOMFORTABLE CONVERSATIONS TO IRON OUT YOUR DIFFERENCES. GET BACK TO LOVING.

THE MOMENT YOU DECIDE TO LIVE AND CLIMB OVER SELF-PITY, EVERY PART OF YOU BEGINS TO AWAKEN.

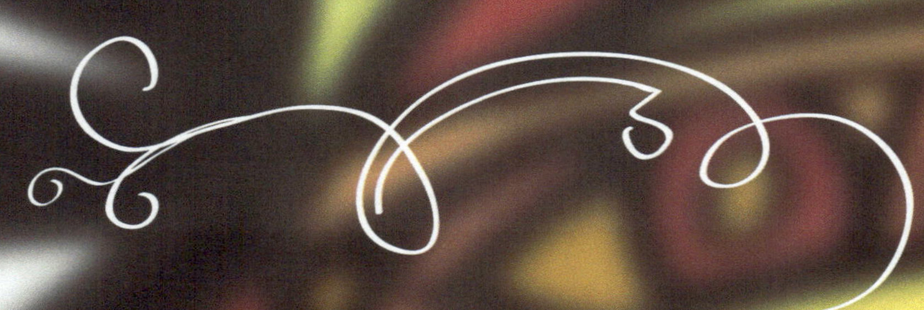

YOU ARE WORTHY
ENOUGH TO ASK
FOR YOUR
HEART'S DESIRES.

SOMEONE KNOWS YOUR STORY AND IS READY TO LOVE YOU IN SPITE OF IT. DON'T COMPROMISE FOR SOMEONE WHO KEEPS REMINDING YOU OF WHO YOU USED TO BE. WAIT FOR SOMEONE WHO HELPS YOU BUILD A BETTER YOU.

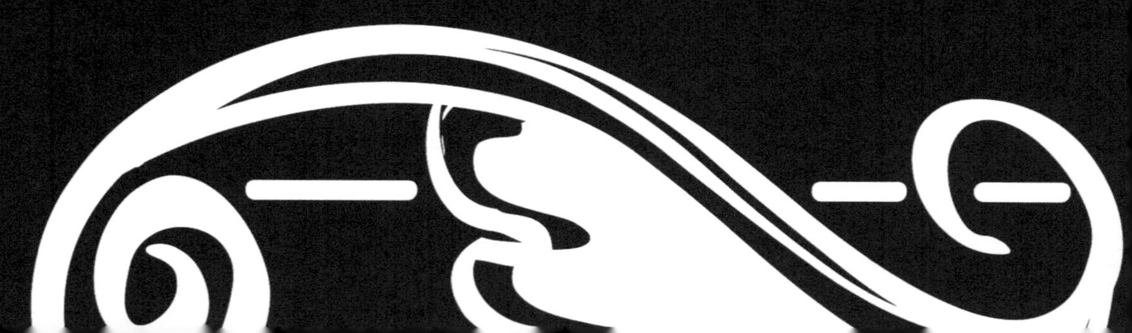

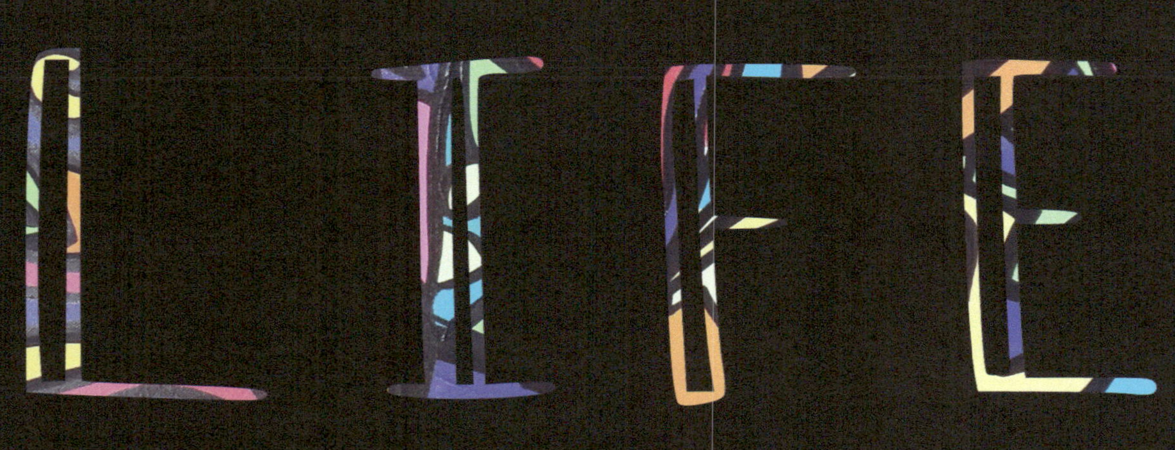
LIFE

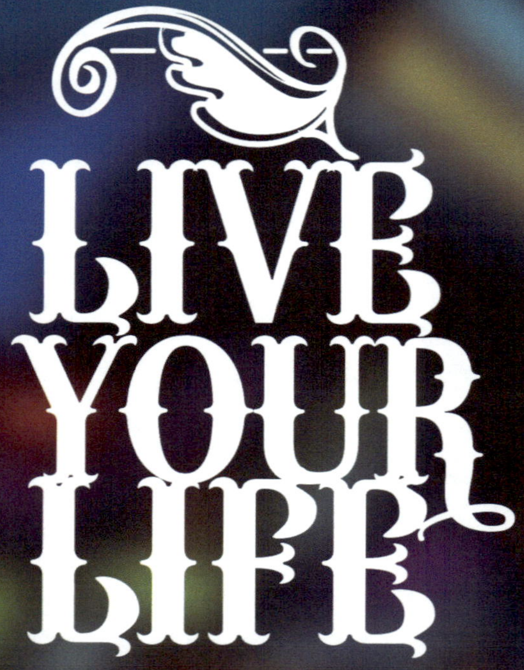

# LIVE YOUR LIFE

as an example of triumph and perseverance. Inspire people by being authentically you. When you look back, you will realize that your story was being written eloquently. Through it all, God is using you to inspire many. Keep going, keep pressing, and keep knowing that everything is a part of His plan.

FORGIVE YOURSELF FOR NOT BEING PERFECT.

The less you resent your process, the quicker you can get through it.

NOTHING
POSITIVE HAPPENS
WITHOUT US SPEAKING
IT REPEATEDLY. IF YOU FEEL LIKE
YOUR WORDS HAVEN'T ACTIVATED
ANYTHING YET, DON'T VERBALIZE YOUR
FRUSTRATIONS. KEEP YOUR POSITIVE
CONFESSIONS IN YOUR HEART AND
ONLY LET POSITIVE WORDS
ESCAPE YOUR
LIPS.

# BEFORE DUMPING

YOUR LOAD ONTO SOMEONE, FIRST CONSIDER WHAT THEY MAY ALREADY BE CARRYING.

A SMILE MAY BE A SIGN OF STRENGTH, NOT HAPPINESS.

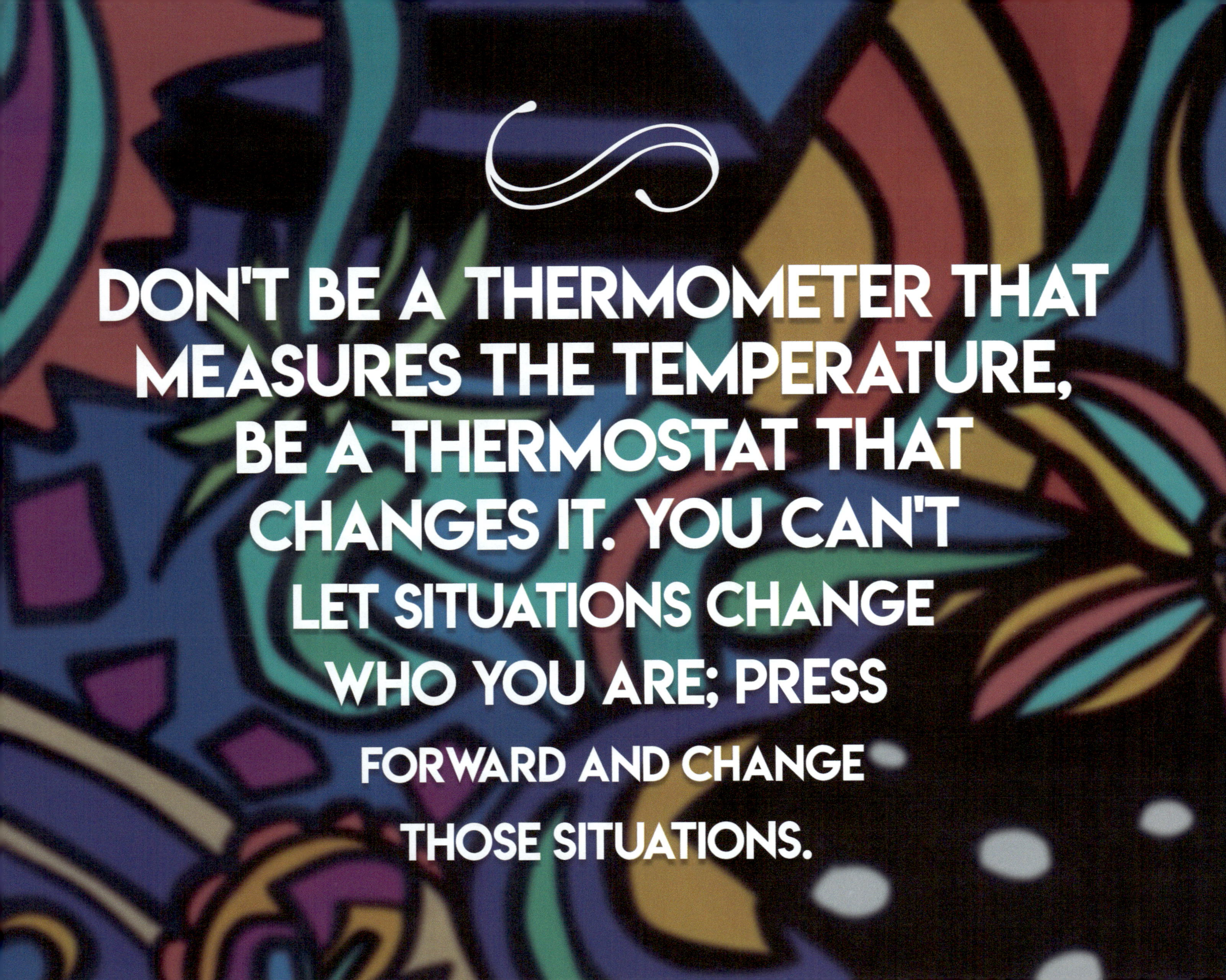
DON'T BE A THERMOMETER THAT MEASURES THE TEMPERATURE, BE A THERMOSTAT THAT CHANGES IT. YOU CAN'T LET SITUATIONS CHANGE WHO YOU ARE; PRESS FORWARD AND CHANGE THOSE SITUATIONS.

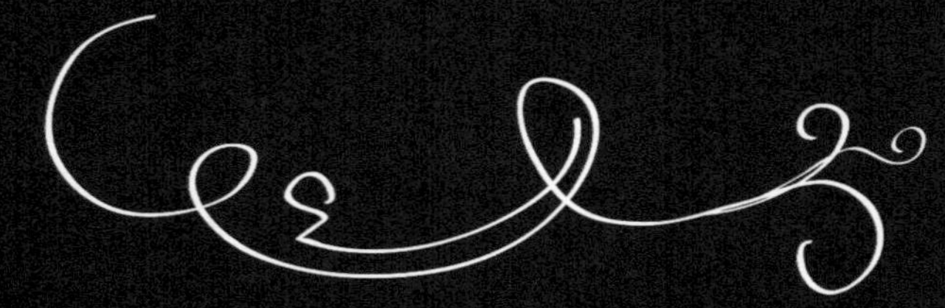

THERE IS GREAT POWER
IN VIEWING LIFE THROUGH
A RETROSPECTIVE LENS.
WHEN YOU LOOK BACK
OVER YOUR LIFE, YOU
WILL SEE GOD'S
DISTINCT HANDIWORK
VERY CLEARLY.

OFTEN TIMES WE ARE IN A RUSH TO GET TO A PLACE THAT GOD HAS ALREADY SET ASIDE AND PROMISED US. ALL WE NEED TO DO IS KEEP LIVING AND BELIEVING GOD.

Be grateful for the revelations, guard your heart, and embrace the process.

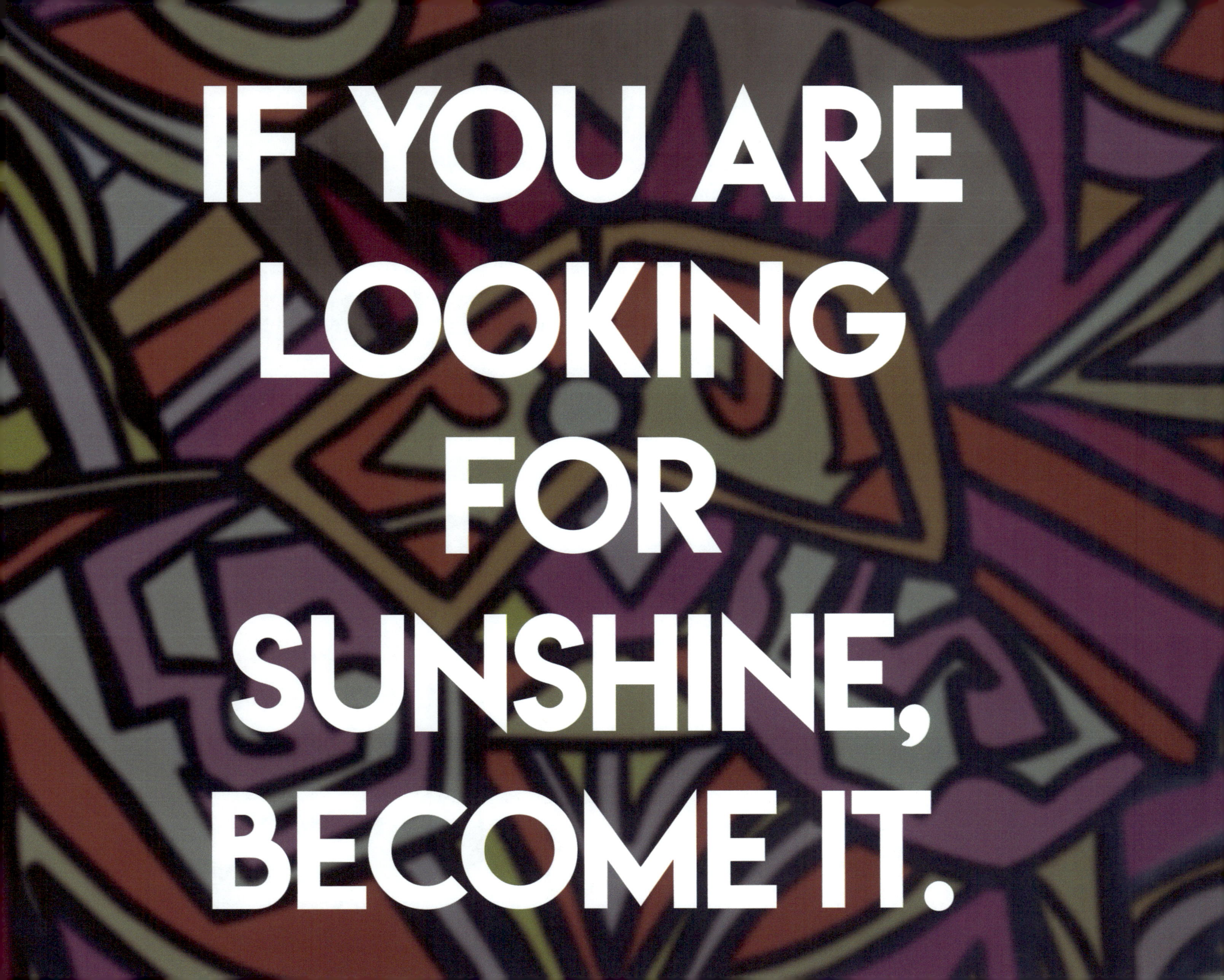

IF YOU ARE LOOKING FOR SUNSHINE, BECOME IT.

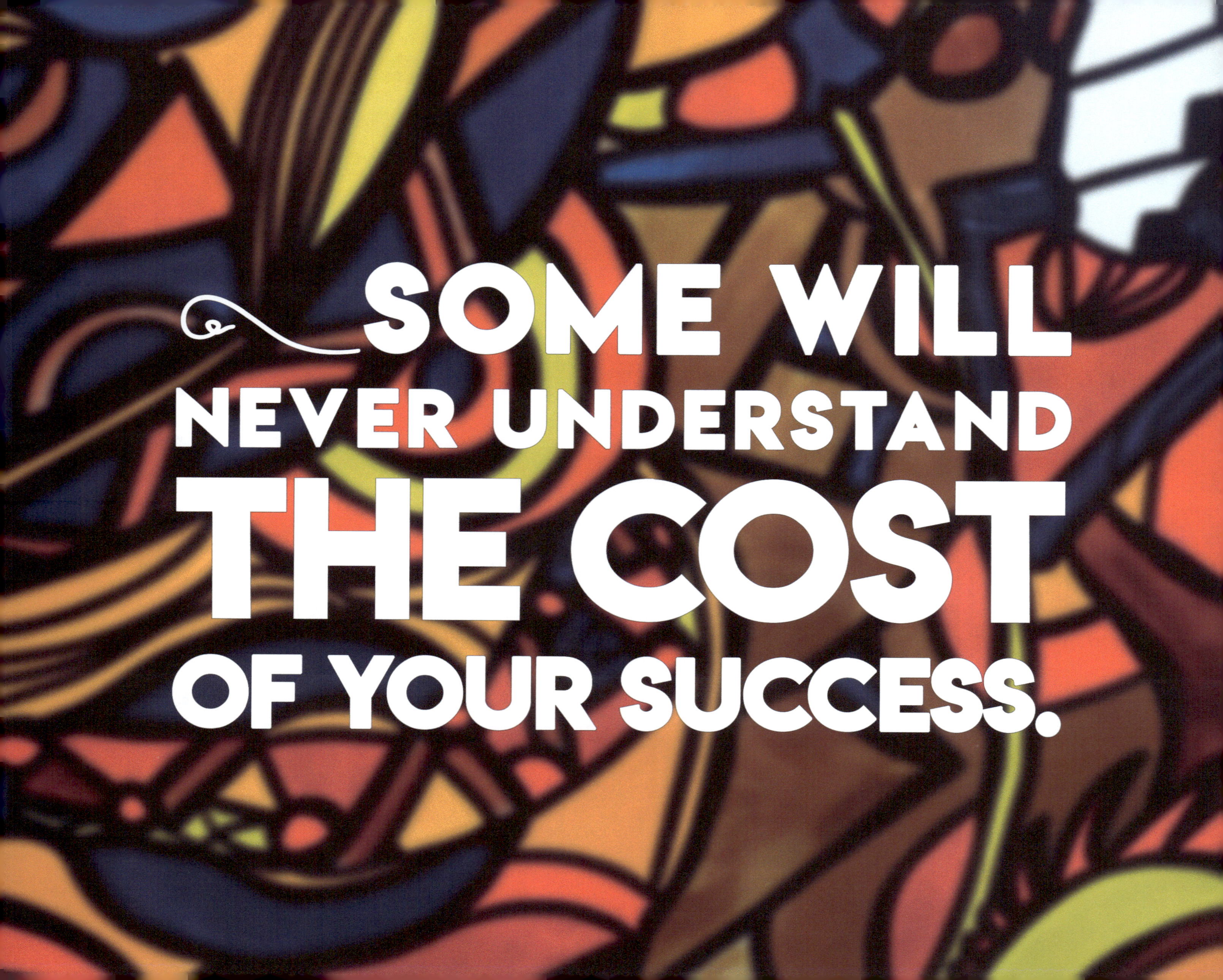

SOME WILL
NEVER UNDERSTAND
THE COST
OF YOUR SUCCESS.

# STOP

## COMPLAINING ABOUT THE JOURNEY AND REMEMBER THE DESTINATION.

ONE
"YES"
MADE EVERY
"NO"
MAKE SENSE.

# MOST PEOPLE ARE LOOKING FOR MIRACLES TO COME IN BIG WAVES, WHEN IN REALITY, WE EXPERIENCE DROPS OF MIRACLES EVERY DAY.

MAKE
THE MOST
OF YOUR
MOMENTS.
YOU'RE
RACING
AGAINST
THE CLOCK.

MOVING AHEAD MEANS YOU'RE LEAVING THE PAST JUST AS IT IS. STOP TRYING TO CHANGE THE RESULTS. YOU CAN ONLY CONTROL THE MOMENT YOU'RE IN RIGHT NOW. LIVE. LOVE. GROW.

**SOMETIMES** YOU HAVE TO LOOK BACK ON WHAT YOU'VE DONE TO KNOW WHAT YOU'RE CAPABLE OF DOING.

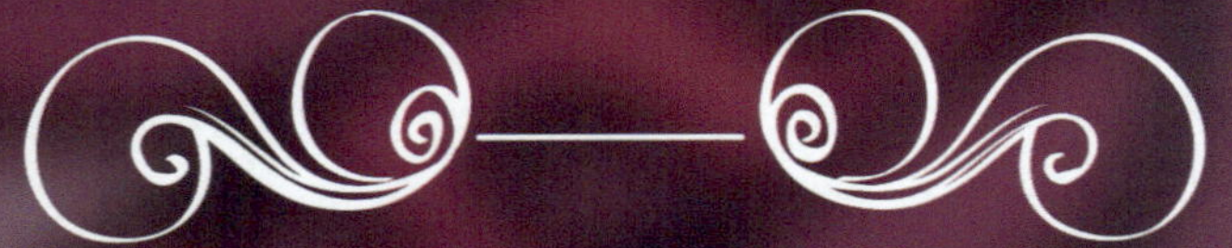

# YOU'VE BEEN DESIGNED ESPECIALLY FOR YOUR JOURNEY. DON'T ENVY YOUR NEIGHBOR'S DESTINATION, BECAUSE YOU DON'T KNOW THEIR PATH. YOU ARE RIGHT WHERE YOU NEED TO BE!

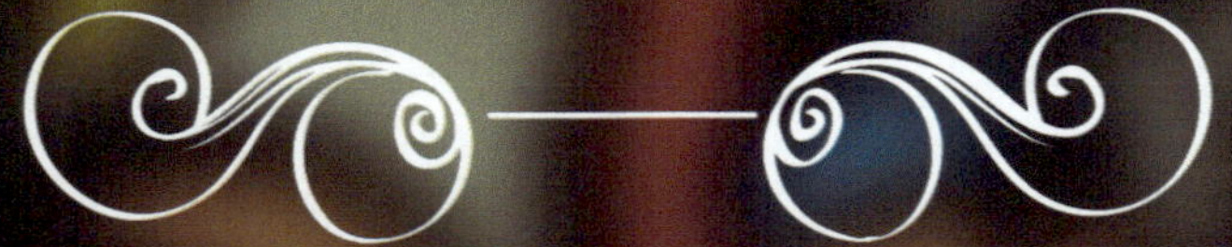

THERE IS POWER IN CONSISTENCY.
WHEN YOU ARE
CONSTANTLY
PRODUCING GREAT THINGS,
YOUR NAME WILL
END UP
IN GREAT PLACES
AND YOUR
GIFT WILL CARVE
A NEW PATH FOR YOU.

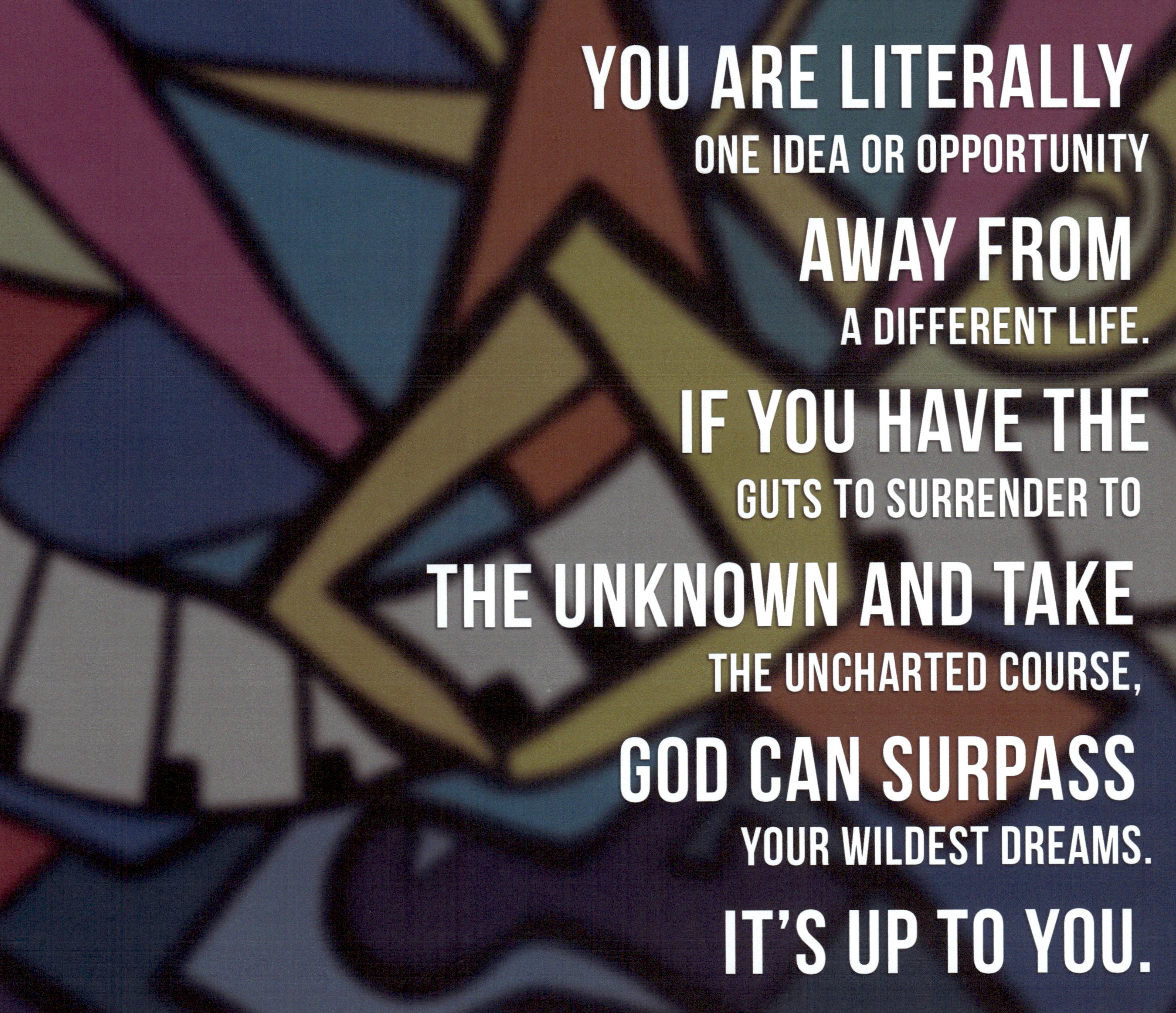

YOU ARE LITERALLY
ONE IDEA OR OPPORTUNITY
AWAY FROM
A DIFFERENT LIFE.
IF YOU HAVE THE
GUTS TO SURRENDER TO
THE UNKNOWN AND TAKE
THE UNCHARTED COURSE,
GOD CAN SURPASS
YOUR WILDEST DREAMS.
IT'S UP TO YOU.

We all have
a distinct purpose
that should be fulfilled.

DON'T BE FOOLED INTO THINKING IT MUST BE
SOMETHING GLAMOROUS OR OVER THE TOP, IT
MIGHT BE SOMETHING SMALL. WHATEVER IT IS, DO
IT WITH EVERY FIBER OF YOUR BEING.

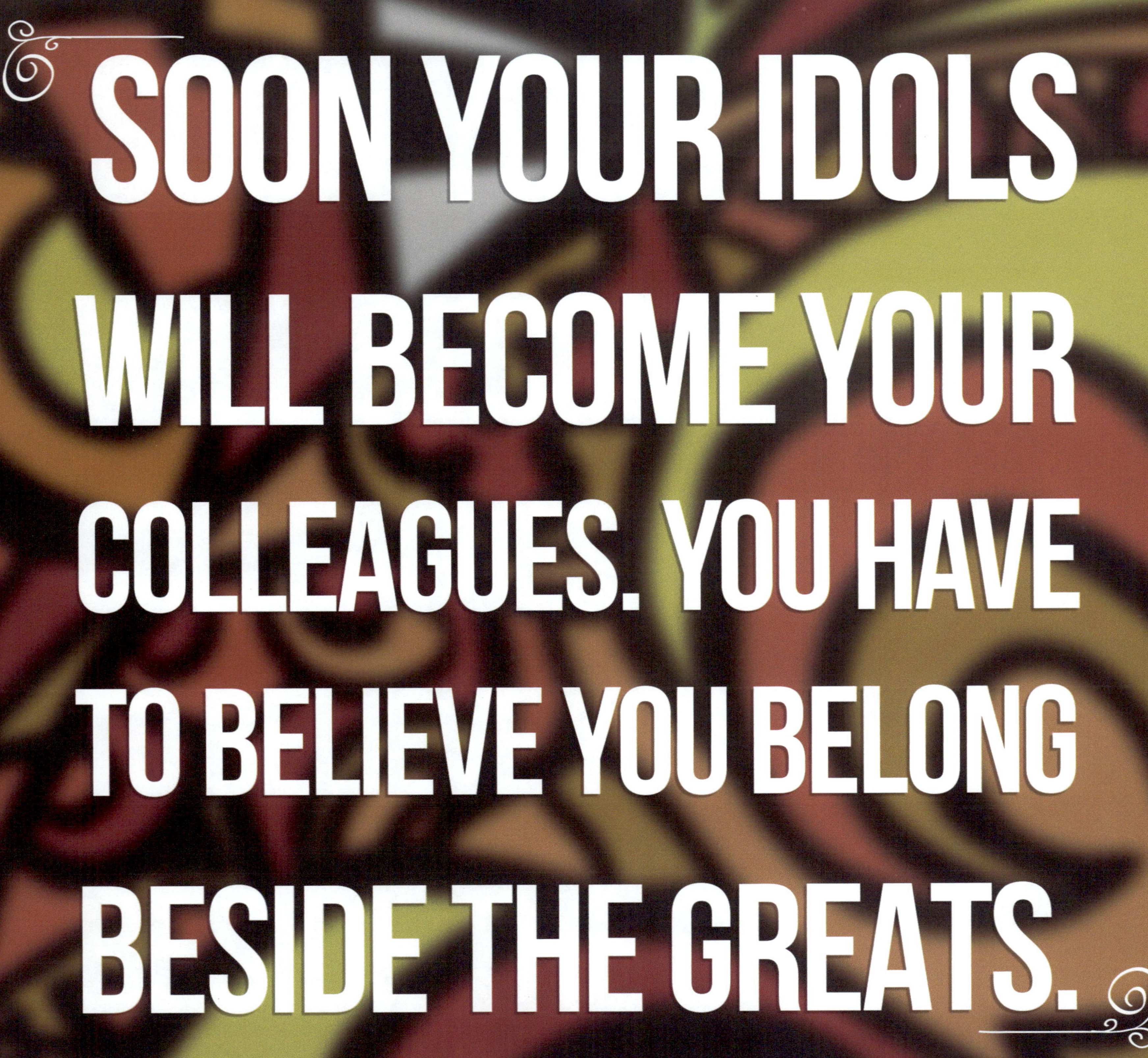

SOON YOUR IDOLS WILL BECOME YOUR COLLEAGUES. YOU HAVE TO BELIEVE YOU BELONG BESIDE THE GREATS.

SPIRIT

Don't talk yourself OUT of your faith.

IF GOD SAID IT AND YOU BELIEVE IT, DON'T ALLOW NEGATIVE THOUGHTS AND WORDS TO COME OUT OF YOU. YOU CAN BE YOUR OWN STUMBLING BLOCK. MAKE THE CONSCIOUS DECISION TO SPEAK LIFE INTO YOUR CIRCUMSTANCES.

YOUR CONSISTENCY IS ATTRACTING ATTENTION. GOD SEES YOUR DILIGENCE AND KNOWS YOUR HEART. DON'T STOP BECAUSE IT FEELS LIKE YOU'RE NOT BEING REWARDED.

SOON, EVERYTHING WILL WORK IN YOUR FAVOR AND YOUR REWARD WILL BE GREATER THAN YOU IMAGINED. GOD HONORS FAITHFULNESS.

God is watching how you react to your circumstances so keep the faith!

# STAY FOCUSED

## BUT TAKE TIME TO

### RELISH IN ALL THAT GOD HAS

#### ALLOWED TO MANIFEST.

AND UNPLUG WHEN NECESSARY.

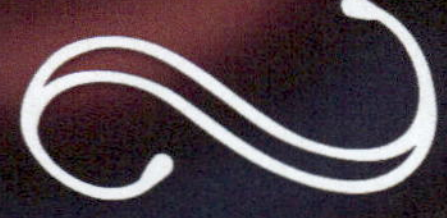

WHEN YOU ARE SET
ASIDE FOR A SPECIFIC PURPOSE,
YOU'RE NO LONGER COMFORTABLE
IN FAMILIAR SETTINGS.

GOD IS CALLING
YOU TO ISOLATE YOURSELF
AND PREPARE FOR THE NEXT LEVEL.
BE OKAY WITH HOW GOD TRANSITIONS
YOU. HE IS VERY DELIBERATE WITH
WHAT HE DOES AND HOW HE DOES IT.

GOD CAN TAKE WHAT'S
EXTRAORDINARY AND MAKE IT
ROUTINE IN YOUR LIFE.
DON'T UNDERESTIMATE GOD'S
POWER TO TOTALLY
TRANSFORM YOUR LIFE IN
AN INSTANT!

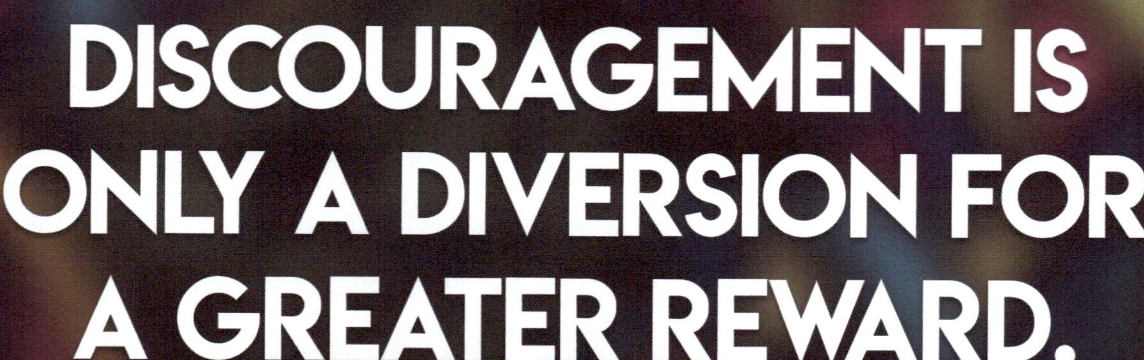

WHEN ONE OPPORTUNITY CLOSES OR DIMINISHES, ANOTHER ONE ARRIVES AND MULTIPLIES.

DISCOURAGEMENT IS ONLY A DIVERSION FOR A GREATER REWARD.

NOTHING HAPPENS OVERNIGHT. IT IS DURING NIGHT THAT YOU ARE TESTED THE MOST. DON'T ALLOW THE SETBACKS TO CONVINCE YOU THAT YOUR TIME ISN'T COMING.

IF YOU CAN ENDURE THROUGH THE NIGHT, YOU ARE PROMISED VICTORY BY DAYBREAK. GOD IS WORKING ON IT AND YOU! YOU ARE TOO CLOSE TO STOP BELIEVING NOW.

BE DETERMINED TO DEMOLISH EVERY NEGATIVE THOUGHT THAT EXALTS ITSELF AGAINST WHAT GOD SAYS ABOUT YOU!

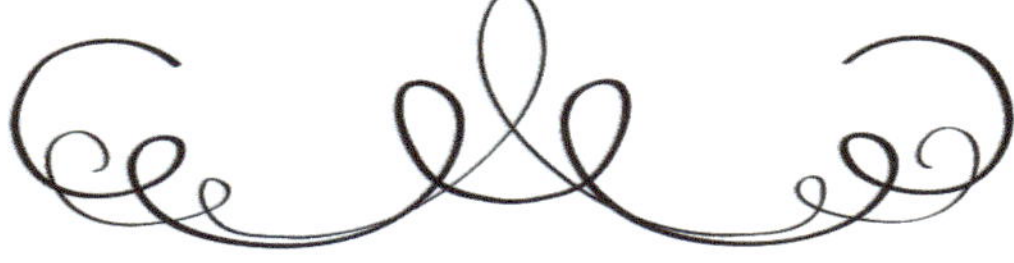

THE FAVOR OF GOD COMES TO YOU IN THE MIDST OF LIFE'S CHALLENGES. WHEN IT SEEMS LIKE ALL THE WORLD AROUND YOU IS TURNING GRAY, KNOW THAT GOD IS STILL ON THE THRONE. HE WILL FIND A WAY FOR HIS LIGHT TO SHINE THROUGH.

When you pray for increase, **DON'T EXPECT IT TO FALL FROM THE SKY.** Instead, expect God to provide opportunities for you to use your talents and generate increase. **WEALTH IS ALREADY IN YOUR HANDS.**

UNTIL YOU GET EVERYTHING OUT OF WHERE YOU ARE, YOU WON'T BE ELEVATED TO WHERE YOU NEED TO BE. DELAY MAY NOT BE A PUNISHMENT, BUT A PROLONGED LESSON.

AT SOME
POINT, YOU
HAVE TO GET OVER
WHATEVER IS HOLDING
YOU BACK FROM LIVING
TO YOUR FULLEST POTENTIAL.
NO PAIN OR MISTREATMENT SHOULD BE
STRONG ENOUGH TO STIFLE YOUR SPIRIT
OR WHO YOU REALLY ARE. PRAY FOR THE
STRENGTH TO FORGIVE AND MOVE
FORWARD. YOU'RE MISSING
VALUABLE MOMENTS TO
LIVE AND LOVE. LET GO
AND WATCH GREAT
THINGS HAPPEN.

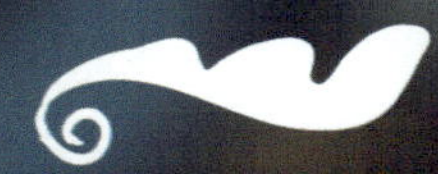

EVEN THE MOST DIFFICULT PUZZLES PIECE TOGETHER TO CREATE A PICTURE. WAIT TO SEE WHAT GOD DOES WITH THE PUZZLE PIECES OF YOUR LIFE. IT'S GOING TO COME TOGETHER JUST FINE.

GOD WILL SEND YOU EXACTLY WHO YOU NEED TO HELP MAKE YOUR DREAMS COME TO LIFE.

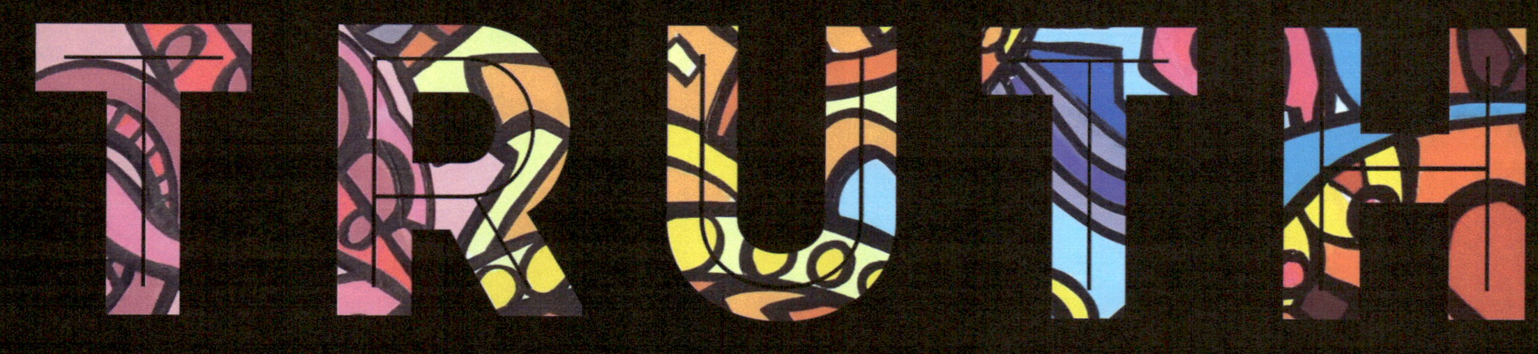
TRUTH

Your words
ARE
currency
AND SO IS
your time.

God doesn't need your permission to use you as an example.

everyone needs a
break. don't
apologize for what
you're entitled to.

Some of the greatest
people in history have
endured some of the
greatest adversities.
So, whatever you're facing,
know that it's a testimony
in the making and press
your way towards
greatness.

GOD
SENDS YOU
WHAT YOU NEED,
NOT ALWAYS
WHAT YOU WANT.
EMBRACE IT EITHER WAY.

SOMETIMES GOD HAS TO EMBARRASS US TO SAVE US.

NOTHING IS A
COINCIDENCE—
EVERYTHING
IS CONNECTED.

YOU DON'T
OWE
EVERYONE
ACCESS
TO YOUR
EMOTIONS.

IT'S BETTER TO BE EXHAUSTED FROM PURSUING PURPOSE AND DOING SOMETHING YOU LOVE, THAN WAKING UP FULLY RESTED TO WALK INTO AN UNFULFILLING PURPOSE AND PERFORMING MUNDANE TASKS.

# S T O P

COMMUNICATING WITH FOLKS WHO DON'T FEED YOUR DREAM OR HELP GUIDE YOU TOWARDS YOUR DESTINY. YOU HAVE NO TIME TO WASTE.

GOD IS STILL PERFECTING YOUR NARRATIVE. DON'T ALLOW OTHER FACTORS TO RUSH YOUR TIMELINE.

SURROUND YOURSELF WITH PEOPLE WHO LOVE GOD AND ARE IN PURSUIT OF THEIR DREAMS. IT'S IMPORTANT TO ASSOCIATE YOURSELF WITH THE RIGHT PEOPLE.

SHOW YOUR RESULTS,
NOT YOUR METHODS.

Everyone doesn't need to know how you got it done, while you're trying to get it done. Just show that it can

Stop feeling the need to explain moves that make sense to you.

FOLLOW YOUR

DREAMS

REGARDLESS OF

WHO IS

FOLLOWING YOU.

THERE

ARE

NO

DAYS OFF

WHEN

EXCELLENCE IS THE

ULTIMATE GOAL.

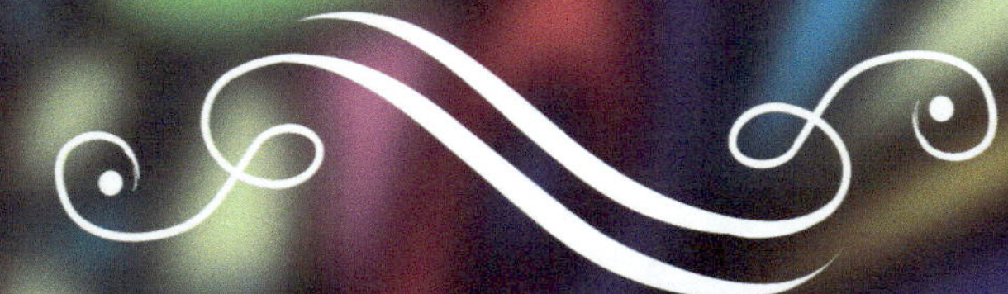

The moment you **decide** to be **fearless** in pursuit of that which makes you **feel** something, you will be forever **free**.

it takes a brave soul to dream and to pursue BiG goals.

PERSON:
GIRL, HOW DO YOU DO IT?

ME:
HOW CAN I NOT? I ASKED FOR THIS OVERFLOW; I WAS BORN FOR THIS MANTLE.

...AND SOMETIMES IT HAPPENS ALL AT ONCE; AFTER IT BEING NOTHING MUCH FOR SO LONG. FAVOR WILL RUSH IN LIKE A FLOOD TO REMIND YOU THAT YOU SERVE THE SAME GOD THAT YOU'VE WITNESSED FOR SO MANY OTHERS. THE SAME GOD KNOWS EVERY NOOK AND CRANNY OF YOUR HEART AND SOUL. THE SAME GOD HAS YOU NEXT IN LINE. THE SAME GOD.

## thank you God

FOR HOLDING BACK WHAT I WASN'T
READY FOR AND PREPARING ME FOR
WHAT YOU'VE ALREADY ALLOWED. MY
UNANSWERED PRAYERS AREN'T YOU
IGNORING ME, YOU JUST WANTED ME
TO SEARCH HARDER FOR YOU.

## thank you

FOR LOVING ME ENOUGH TO SAY NO
TO THINGS THAT AREN'T YOUR WILL
FOR ME AND OPENING DOORS
THAT I NEVER IMAGINED.
FOREVER GRATEFUL.

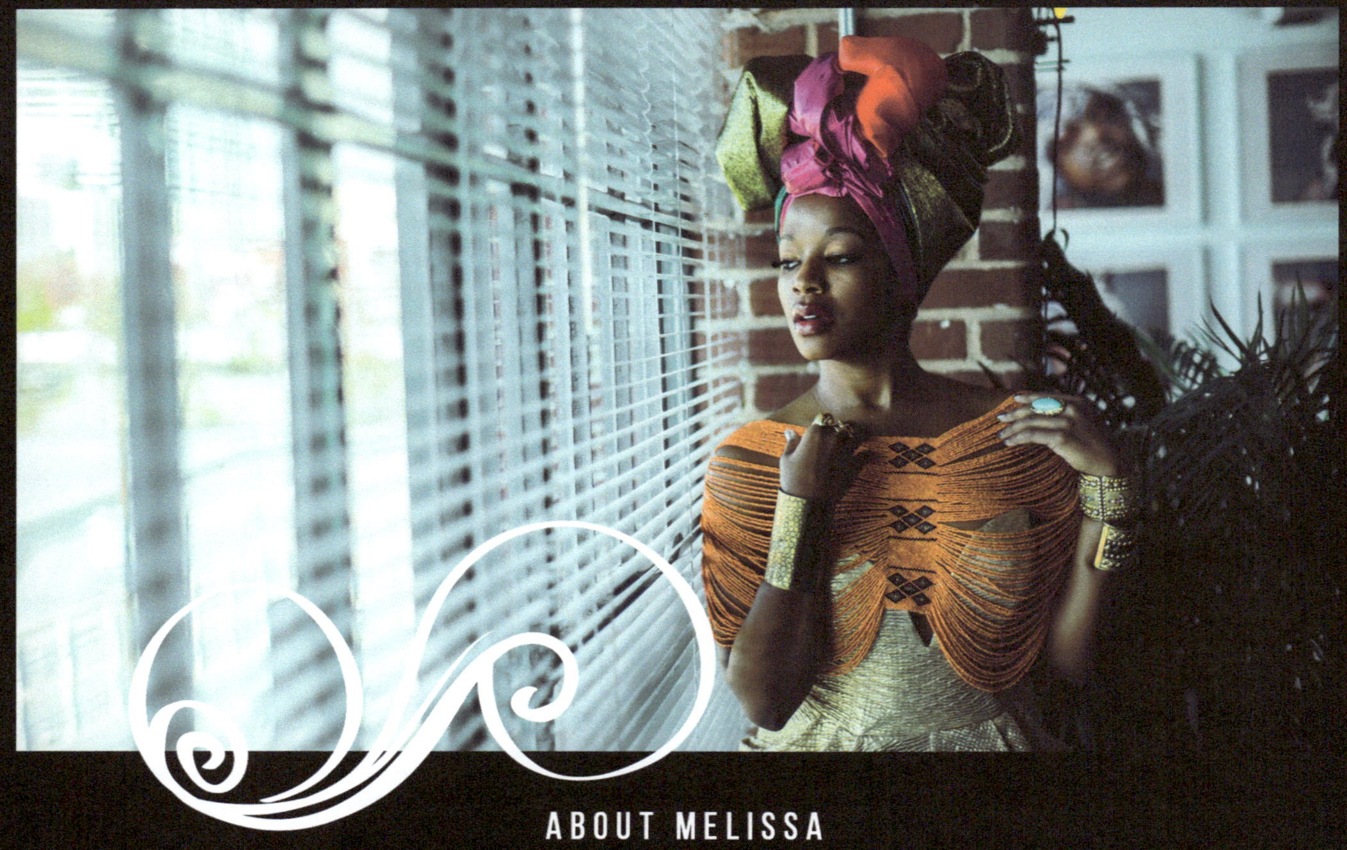



Melissa Mitchell is an Atlanta-based abstract creator with a love of vibrant colors, unique shapes, and bold, dark lines. As a self-taught artist, she pulls inspiration from her Bahamian heritage, melodic tunes, and the colorful world around her. Since February 2014, she has created over 400 original art pieces, painted 40 larger than life murals, sold thousands of artistic creations globally, partnered with several Fortune 500 brands, and been featured in an array of multi-media campaigns. She aims to create pieces that evoke emotion, to serve as a "light source," speak to the soul, but above all—inspire people to follow their passions and cultivate their dreams.

Melissa believes, *"Art is like love. You make it what you want and it makes you feel things you can't always describe; you're left to just relish in the beauty of it. Art has single-handedly changed my life and the way I live it."*

Melissa Mitchell's optimistic lens and innovative talents have propelled her to heights she never imagined. She attributes her greatness to a creative father and a faith-filled mother. Melissa is driven by the fact that she never wants to leave this earth without knowing she made a significant impact. Her ultimate goal is to live a life of example and become a philanthropist and world-renowned creator.

# ACKNOWLEDGEMENTS

Sometimes, God hides the answers you seek in plain sight, while other answers require more of a quest. He will reveal things to you in an instant, and some other truths are revealed by just living. I have learned that there is no cookie-cutter way to live, you just have to commit to waking up each day and LIVE IT. This book serves as a view from my kaleidoscope, as I find my way closer to the Source. On my journey, I have been blessed with some of the greatest souls in the universe to keep me going.

To my mother, I thank you for filling me with faith big enough to see beyond my current circumstances and always reminding me of my purpose. Thank you for giving me the courage to be me. Thank you for letting me wear as many colors as I want, being my voice of reason, a shoulder to cry on, and for teaching me how to be a Queen. If I'm half the woman you are, I will be an undeniable force in this universe. To my father, who taught me to leave a legacy with every word I speak, I thank you for teaching me how to be a creative giant, a fearless innovator, and an intentional human being. Thank you for showing me how to monetize my tears and how to forgive in order to elevate. Your memory and name will forever live on. To my sister Mo, thank you for teaching me how to be bold with my delivery and soft with my love. To my sister Mel, thank you for teaching me to find humor in everything and showing me what perseverance looks like.

To Trease, thank you for reminding me of my Bahamian heritage and letting me know it's okay to celebrate being beautiful every single day. To Auntie Nina, thank you for teaching me to be forever young and to enjoy life. To all of my family, thank you for cheering me on and being my biggest fans. It's an honor to be related. To my ancestors, I honor each of you and carry your spirits with me. It is my duty to make the world know the greatness of our lineage and be the fruition of dreams deferred.

To my closest friends, thank you for putting up with me over the years and never loving me any less. I don't know where I would be without each of you. It's not easy loving a creative but somehow you all keep me around. I love y'all long time.

To T and Tali, thank you for being my spiritual partners, my sanity, and my prayer warriors. Thank you for reminding me of my worth daily.

To Ash, thank you for always giving me the real, even when I don't want it. Thank you for laughing until we cry, calling me when Dillard's has a sale, and for loving me through every season. To Steph, thank you for standing in faith with me, persevering through life's changes by my side, and for being like real family. To Ri and Krys, thank you for always having my back, loving me through my ups and downs, for dancing real nasty at parties with me, and for growing with me through the years. To Ry, thank you for capturing every perfect shot throughout my creative career.

To H2, thank you for teaching me how to slow down enough to listen to the universe and how to decode life's messages. I love you forever for who you pushed me to become. To my deaconess circle, thank you for being a text message away and for reminding me to remain focused in this jumbled up world. My Virgo love runs deep. To my squad, thank you for being my escape throughout the day. To all of my friends who push me daily, thank you each for loving me in a special way. To my mentors, thank you for seeing something in me even when I couldn't. To you Renita, thank you for pushing greatness out of me and helping me to stay on task. I would not be who I am without each of you.

To my FAMUly, thank you for supporting me from day 1. It's an honor and a privilege to be a Rattler. I certainly want to extend a HUGE thank you to everyone who has supported me from the beginning. When I doubted my talent and my journey, I was always met with love, encouragement, and ORDERS. I am forever grateful for the relentless support over the years.

I even want to thank the no's, the disappointments, the failed love attempts, and the heartaches. Everything that hasn't happened has allowed so much to be born from within. Everything I'm not has made me who I am. I'm grateful for the journey, the lessons, and the personal evolution.

This book is dedicated: to every dreamer who put down a dream, for every little girl who was told she wears too many colors, to every person who thinks they won't ever fit in, to everybody who has been told NO too many times to count, this book is for us. After you look through my kaleidoscope, perhaps you will dream a little bigger and live a little louder. We only get one life to live, so you might as well have the courage to be you. If you want something different in life, be prepared to do things differently. Simple enough right?

Never stop living.
Never stop being.
Never stop loving.
Never stop doing.

Just be authentically you and the rest will sort itself out later.


~Melissa

To learn more about Melissa A. Mitchell and Abeille Creations, visit
www.MelissaAMitchell.com.